THE WORK OF DR EDWARD BACH
An Introduction and Guide
to the 38 Flower Remedies

CONTENTS

FOREWORD	3
INTRODUCTION	4
WHAT ARE THE FLOWER REMEDIES?	5
DR EDWARD BACH	6
CHOOSING AND USING THE REMEDIES	9
THE REMEDIES AND THEIR USES	11
RESCUE REMEDY	50
CHOOSING REMEDIES FOR CHILDREN	52
CHOOSING REMEDIES FOR ANIMALS AND PLANTS	53
FURTHER INFORMATION	53

FOREWORD

This booklet is a general guide, introducing the reader to the work of Dr Edward Bach. It is ideal for those new to flower therapy, offering straightforward descriptions of the remedies and other practical information, to help use the remedies in everyday situations.

Those who wish to use the remedies to full effect are encouraged to study the benefits in more detail. At the back of the book you will find a full list of recommended literature for further reading, together with details of video and audio cassette tapes.

Dr Bach's philosophy is one of simplicity and this was reflected in his way of life, style of living and in his final completed work - the 38 flower remedies which gently ease distress and combat ill-health by enabling harmony and peace to flood our lives.

He enjoyed the simple pleasures in life, and during the last years of his life, spent at his home, Mount Vernon, he would enjoy the garden where many remedy plants still grow to this day, making furniture for the cottage and getting to know the local villagers.

He lived at Mount Vernon with his two devoted colleagues - Nora Weeks and Victor Bullen - who, at his request, looked after his work and continued to prepare his remedies for some 44 years, until Nora's death in 1978. They too had loyal and trusted partners to whom the continuation of the doctor's work was in turn passed down. John Ramsell has been fully involved at Mount Vernon since 1971. Having worked alongside Nora and Victor for several years, he gained a unique insight, and was personally taught and appointed by Nora Weeks. I joined my father in 1985, and we now run the Bach Centre, Mount Vernon, together.

The preparation of the mother tinctures has always been conducted by the Trustees of Mount Vernon and to this day, Dr Bach's original locations are still used. Mount Vernon is also the Centre for Education and regular courses are held to establish a register of professional therapists, doctors and counsellors who incorporate the remedies in their work. In addition, introductory seminars and workshops are organised at special venues throughout the country.

Since Dr Bach's death in 1936, his personal belongings and writings have been housed in the archives at Mount Vernon. The house itself is full of the doctor's hand-made furniture. We are most concerned that the Centre remain intact for all time, a wish that Dr Bach himself expressed, and to this end, a Charitable Trust and Educational Foundation were established and the ownership of the house, land and all that is embodied therein were transferred to the auspices of the Trust, thereby ensuring that Mount Vernon will be protected for all time.

The work, and the house itself, remain to this day virtually unaltered. All of us, past and present, who have been privileged to carry on Dr Bach's work, have diligently upheld its purity and originality and thereby ensured that the quality and untarnished reputation of such a dedicated and humble, yet extraordinarily gifted man, remain intact.

Dr Bach believed that this simple system of healing would be the medicine of the future. As time goes on, more and more people find, use and benefit from his gentle remedies and one day, when they can be found in every home and considered as vital as sticking plaster, his dream and hopes for us all will have come true.

Judy Howard,
Co-Trustee and Curator
The Dr. Edward Bach Centre
Mount Vernon, Sotwell, Wallingford, Oxon, England

INTRODUCTION

'Health depends on being in harmony with our souls.' Dr. Edward Bach

Dr Edward Bach, M.B., B.S., M.R.C.S., L.R.C.P., D.P.H. (the name is correctly pronounced 'Batch') was a Physician and Homoeopath, who spent his life searching for the purest methods of healing.

He believed, as many doctors do today, that attitude of mind plays a vital role in maintaining health and recovering from illness. When he died in 1936 he had developed a complete system of 38 flower remedies, each prepared from the flowers of wild plants, trees or bushes. They work by treating the individual rather than the disease or its symptoms.

Today, these safe, gentle remedies are used world-wide by private individuals, medical and complementary health practitioners, psychotherapists, counsellors, dentists, vets and healers. Over the years the Bach Centre at Mount Vernon in Oxfordshire has received thousands of testimonials from patients and practitioners vouching for their effectiveness.

The purpose of the remedies is to support the patient's fight against illness by addressing the depression, anxiety, trauma and other emotional factors that are thought to impede physical healing. They can also be used preventively, at times of anxiety and stress, and are particularly helpful for the many people who feel generally tired and unwell without a specific medical diagnosis.

The remedies may be taken on their own or in conjunction with medical or other treatment; they will not conflict with medication, including homoeopathic remedies. The remedies are completely safe, have no unwanted side effects and are non-addictive. They are gentle in action and can safely be taken by people of all ages from new-born babies to elderly people. They are also beneficial for animals and plants.

It is important to note that they are not intended as a substitute for medical treatment; should symptoms persist, you are advised to consult your medical practitioner.

WHAT ARE THE FLOWER REMEDIES?

'Health is our heritage, our right. It is the complete and full union between soul, mind and body; and this is not a difficult far-away ideal to attain, but one so easy and natural that many of us have overlooked it.' Dr Edward Bach

Dr Bach discovered 38 remedies, each for a specific emotional and mental state, plus a combination of five of the remedies designed for difficult and demanding situations, which he called Rescue Remedy.

37 of the 38 are based on single wild flowers and tree blossoms. The exception, Rock Water, is made from the water of a natural spring with healing properties.

How do they work?

These flower remedies, like other forms of natural medicine, take effect by treating the individual, not disease or the symptoms of the disease. They work specifically on the emotional condition of the person concerned. Thus two people, with the same complaint, eg arthritis, may benefit from quite different remedies. One may be resigned to the illness, while the other may be impatient with it, so different remedies will be appropriate in each case.

The effect of taking the remedies is not to suppress negative attitudes but to transform them into positive ones, stimulating one's own potential for self-healing and freeing the physical system to engage fully in fighting disease and stress.

People do not have to be physically ill to benefit from the remedies. Many of us go through times of difficulty and fatigue when negativity creeps in; at these times the remedies are invaluable in restoring the balance before physical symptoms appear.

Do they have a placebo effect?

No more than any other medicines. The remedies are very effective with both animals and babies, as well as in helping sceptical people who try them as a last resort. Plants also benefit from the remedies; gardeners find that giving Rescue Remedy on re-potting, for example, helps the plants to flourish after being moved.

How long will they keep?

Remedies in their concentrated form can be kept for up to five years.

DR EDWARD BACH

Dr Edward Bach(1886-1936) was a physician well ahead of his time. In his short career he moved from orthodox medicine into developing a natural form of medicine to treat emotional and spiritual health, very much in tune with the trends in natural health in the 1990s.

Born in Moseley outside Birmingham, of Welsh extraction, he was an intuitive, delicate but independent child with a great love of nature. He left school aged 16 and spent three years in his father's Birmingham brass foundry, in order to pay for his own medical training.

Dr Bach's early medical career was both conventional and successful. In 1912 he qualified at University College Hospital (UCH), London where he became Casualty Medical Officer in 1913; later that year he became Casualty House Surgeon at the National Temperance Hospital. After recovering from a breakdown in health, he developed a busy practice close to Harley Street.

From an early age, Dr Bach had been aware that people's personality and attitudes have an effect on their state of health. As a student he took an interest in patients as people rather than cases and early on came to the conclusion that, in illness, personality is more important than symptoms and should be taken into account in medical treatment.

He became increasingly dissatisfied with the limitations of orthodox medicine and its focus on curing symptoms. Believing that effective treatment involves addressing the *causes* of illness, he decided to pursue an interest in immunology and became Assistant Bacteriologist at UCH in 1915.

His health was never robust; refused for service in World War I, he worked himself to illness in 1917, and was expected to die. His determination to complete his work led to a complete recovery and when he later developed his remedies, he was strongly influenced by the belief that following one's true vocation is essential to spiritual and physical health.

From 1919-22 he worked as a pathologist and bacteriologist at the London Homoeopathic Hospital. There he was struck by the fact that Samuel Hahnemann, the founder of homoeopathy, had recognised the importance of personality in disease 150 years before. Combining these principles with his knowledge of orthodox medicine, he developed the Seven Bach Nosodes, oral vaccines based on intestinal bacteria which purified the intestinal tract with remarkable effects on patients' general health, and on difficult chronic conditions like arthritis.

He still had his Harley Street practice, and treated the poor for no payment in Nottingham Place. With his little spare time, he continued to search for simpler and purer methods of healing. Although the medical profession had adopted his vaccines (they are still used today by some homoeopathic and other physicians), he disliked the fact that they were based on bacteria and was anxious to replace these with gentler methods, possibly based on plants.

In 1928, at a dinner party, he had a revelation. Looking at his fellow guests, he realised that they fell into several distinct types. From this, he came to the inspired conclusion that each type would react to illness in a particular way. That autumn he visited Wales and brought back two plants, Mimulus and Impatiens; he prepared these as he did the oral vaccines, and prescribed them according to his patients' personality, with immediate and successful results. Later that year he added Clematis. With these three remedies he was on the brink of developing an entirely new system of medicine.

In the spring of 1930, aged 43, Dr Bach closed his laboratory and his lucrative practice and went to Wales to seek further remedies in nature. Walking through a dew-laden field early one morning, it struck him that each dewdrop, heated by the sun, would acquire the healing properties of the plant it lay on. This inspired him to develop a method of preparing remedies using pure water.

Later that year he wrote the short book *Heal Thyself*, with its message that physical disease is the result of being at odds with one's spiritual purpose. It was published in 1931 and has remained in print ever since.

From August 1930 until 1934 Dr Bach based himself in Cromer, on the Norfolk coast, finding and preparing further flower remedies, and successfully treating patients with them.

Dr Bach charged no fees, and his financial resources were dwindling. In 1934 he moved to Mount Vernon, the small house in Oxfordshire which is still the Dr Edward Bach Centre. He worked on, writing, treating patients in Sotwell and London and continuing his search for further remedies. During this time he suffered considerably both mentally and physically before finding the plant to relieve his symptoms.

He continued to work and lecture, while training assistants to carry on his work. Once he had developed 38 remedies, together with the Rescue Remedy, he knew that no further remedies were needed; the 38 remedies covered all aspects of human nature and thus all the negative states of mind underlying illness.

At the end of November 1936, he died in his sleep, content that his mission was complete. He entrusted full responsibility for the continuation of his work to develop friends and colleagues, whom he had trained. He also requested that his home should remain the source of his findings. So, still today, carried through by direct succession, the Bach Centre Mount Vernon is actively involved in advice and education and continues to prepare the mother tinctures. The Trustees thereby ensure that the traditions and principles of purity, simplicity and completeness are maintained.

RECOMMENDED BOOKS: *The Medical Discoveries of Edward Bach* (Weeks)
The Story of Mount Vernon (Howard)
VIDEO: *The Light that Never Goes Out* – the Story of Dr Bach's Life

Dr Bach's Philosophy

Dr Bach's philosophy was at once simple and profound, based on the innate perfection and spiritual nature of human beings. Disease is 'entirely the result of a conflict between our spiritual and mortal selves.' Health and happiness result from being in harmony with our own nature, and doing the work for which we are individually suited.

As he wrote:

'It means doing the house-keeping, painting, farming, acting, or serving our fellow-men in shops and houses. And this work, whatever it may be, if we love it above all else, is... the work we have to do in this world, and in which alone we can be our true selves.'

'Disease is the re-action to interferences. This is temporary failure and unhappiness and this occurs when we allow others to interfere with our purpose in life and implant in our minds doubt, or fear, or indifference.'

Dr Bach divided the 38 remedies into seven groups, representing fundamental conflicts which prevent us from being true to ourselves:–

- Fear
- Uncertainty
- Insufficient interest in present circumstances
- Loneliness
- Over-sensitivity to influences and ideas
- Despondency or despair
- Over-care for the welfare of others

Within each group, the remedies each cover a specific nature of the difficulty concerned. For example, fear may take the form of terror, (requiring Rock Rose), definable, everyday fears (Mimulus), fear of losing one's mind (Cherry Plum), inexplicable fears (Aspen), or fears for other people (Red Chestnut).

Just as Dr Bach identified the seven areas of conflict which interfere with our health, so he defined the stages in the healing of disease, ... Peace, Hope, Joy, Faith, Certainty, Wisdom, Love.

RECOMMENDED BOOKS: *Heal Thyself* (Bach)
(See page 54)   *Original Writings of Edward Bach* (Ramsell/Howard)

CHOOSING AND USING THE REMEDIES

Pages 12-50 of this booklet give descriptions of the 38 remedies and Rescue Remedy and the emotional and mental conditions for which each is needed, together with the positive potential of the patient once harmony is restored.

It is possible that more than one remedy may be suitable for your case; if so, you can combine up to 6 or 7 remedies if necessary.

When you are first familiarising yourself with the remedies, it can seem that a great many apply to you, and people have asked why they should not use all 38 remedies together. However, Dr Bach tested out a composite of this kind and found it unsatisfactory. Experience over time enables prescribers to become very accurate in pinpointing the most salient remedies.

Clarifying your choice

The descriptions of the states for which the remedies are recommended are not always flattering, and it may be hard to recognise yourself in them. These are descriptions of extreme negative states; reading the 'Positive Potential' of each remedy will help you to appreciate the balance.

Since it is not always easy to see ourselves, it can be helpful to ask a friend for an opinion, preferably someone objective rather than a partner or close relative who may be emotionally involved with your problems.

Finding the root cause

In choosing your remedies, it helps to look for the root cause of your particular problem. For example, if you have a problem of addiction (to alcohol, cigarettes, chocolate, etc.) you will see that Agrimony may be helpful, particularly for people who use addictions to escape from problems. First, check under Agrimony to see whether the characteristics of Agrimony apply to you. If they do, you should then ask yourself from what you are escaping.

Behind the cheerful front of the Agrimony personality there may be a childhood trauma (for which Star of Bethlehem would be suitable), fear (Mimulus or Aspen), hatred (Holly) or resentment (Willow), among other possibilities. The appropriate remedy can be taken together with Agrimony.

Will it harm me if I pick the wrong remedy?

No. The remedies cannot be harmful, and if you pick an inappropriate one, it will simply not have an effect.

Directions for use

Once the remedy or combination of remedies has been chosen, take two drops in a cup of water and sip at intervals, or two drops of each chosen remedy in a 30ml bottle of mineral water and from this take four drops four times a day until relief is obtained. It is quite safe to take these as often as needed. Hold the dose in the mouth for a few moments before swallowing.

In the case of Rescue Remedy the dosage instructions are slightly different and are as follows: four drops in water sipped at intervals or four drops directly on the tongue (see page 51).

Drops can be added to a baby's bottle or a child's fruit juice.

NOTE: The remedies can be taken alongside medication, including homoeopathic remedies, without any interference at all.

For fluctuating moods
For daily ups and downs such as temporary tiredness or frustration, a few drops of the appropriate remedy can be taken in a cup of water, fruit juice, tea or any other drink, and sipped fairly frequently.

Taking the drops undiluted
If no liquid is available you can take two drops direct from the stock bottle (four drops in the case of Rescue Remedy), though please note that this will mean a direct intake of alcohol. Avoid contact between the dropper and your mouth for hygienic reasons.

For emergencies
In the case of difficult and stressful situations or startling experiences, see the Rescue Remedy, pages 51-52.

For how long should I take them?

The time taken for the remedies to have a noticeable effect varies according to individuals and circumstances. If you are experiencing a sudden onset of depression, for instance, you may observe immediate results after taking two drops of Mustard. Similarly, if you wake up one day with a typical 'Monday morning' feeling, sipping some Hornbeam in water should enable you to face the day with calm energy.

On the other hand, if the emotional state is deep-rooted, it may take some days or weeks before you notice a difference. However the people around may well see changes much earlier. As a rule, the remedies work undramatically and gently; the change happens at a natural pace to which people easily adjust.

When you begin to experience physical and emotional relief, it may be time to stop taking the remedies.

If there is no improvement after taking the remedies for a fortnight, reconsider the choice of remedies; there may be an aspect you have missed. If only a small change has occurred, continue to take them or consider whether an additional remedy could be added to the combination.

It frequently happens that after taking one set of remedies for a month or so, it becomes clear that there are other aspects of the personality in need of healing, and a different remedy or combination of remedies is called for.

Reactions

The remedies have no adverse side effects. However, like other forms of natural medicine, they may allow suppressed symptoms to surface. These could include such things as rashes while the body is being cleared of toxins, or an awareness of emotions which have been denied expression. These are an important part of the healing process and are only temporary.

RECOMMENDED BOOKS: *The Twelve Healers & Other Remedies* (Bach)
The Bach Flower Remedies Step by Step (Howard)
The Handbook of the Bach Flower Remedies (Chancellor)
Questions & Answers (Ramsell)
Bach Flower Therapy (Scheffer)
VIDEO: *Bach Flower Remedies: A Further Understanding*
AUDIO CASSETTE: *Getting to know the Bach Flower Remedies.*

(See pages 54 - 56)

THE REMEDIES AND THEIR USES

In the following pages the 38 remedies are listed alphabetically, together with the situations for which they are recommended, and the potential of the personality once harmony has been restored.

They are not used directly for physical complaints, but for the sufferer's worry, apprehension, hopelessness, irritability etc., because these states of mind or moods not only hinder recovery of health and retard convalescence but are generally accepted as causes of sickness and disease.

AGRIMONY
Agrimonia Eupatoria

Keywords: MENTAL TORMENT BEHIND A BRAVE FACE

People who need Agrimony often appear carefree and humourous, but their *joie de vivre* is a mask for anxieties, worries and even real inner torment, which they may be trying to conceal from themselves as well as others. If in pain or discomfort, they are likely to joke about it, unwilling to express their real fears. They dislike being alone and are very sociable, seeking company as a distraction. They try to ignore the darker side of life, and prefer to make light of things rather than enter into a confrontation. They may also suffer from restlessness at night, with churning thoughts (*see also White Chestnut*).

Agrimony people may suppress their discomfort with the aid of heavy drinking, or the use of drugs or comfort eating.

The positive potential of Agrimony is for those who are genuinely cheerful and good company, communicate their real feelings openly and can accept that life has its less pleasant side. Their cheerfulness stems from a real sense of self-acceptance and inner joy; they see problems in perspective and are diplomatic peacemakers.

ASPEN
Populus Tremula

Keywords: FEARS AND WORRIES OF UNKNOWN ORIGIN

Aspen is indicated for people who are seized by sudden fears or worries for no specific reason, and who may therefore be generally nervy and anxious. A typical need for Aspen is on wakening in fear from a bad dream, even if the dream itself is forgotten. Aspen is helpful for young children experiencing nightmares and night terrors (*see also Rock Rose*).

Aspen fears can occur during day or night; an inexplicable anxiety or sense of foreboding may strike when alone, or suddenly in the company of friends.

These sudden unexplained attacks of terror may be accompanied by sweating or trembling.

The positive potential of Aspen is a state of inner peace, security and fearlessness. Apprehension is replaced by a desire for adventure and new experiences, disregarding difficulties and dangers.

Aspen enables people to realise that everything is supported by love. As Dr Bach wrote: 'Once we come to that realisation, we are beyond pain and suffering, beyond care or worry or fear, beyond everything except the joy of life, the joy of death, and the joy of our immortality... we can walk that path through any danger, through any difficulty unafraid.'

BEECH
Fagus Sylvatica

Keywords: INTOLERANCE

Beech is for people who are constantly making criticisms, intolerant of other people's shortcomings and unable to make allowances. They have a strong sense of their own superiority, can be judgmental and arrogant and are easily irritated by other people's mannerisms or habits. They are convinced that they are always in the right and everyone else in the wrong (*see also Impatiens*).

The positive potential of Beech is tolerance and a sense of compassion for and unity with others; the positive Beech person can see the good in others despite their imperfections, supported by the knowledge that everyone is working towards perfection in their unique way.

CENTAURY
Centaurium Umbellatum

Keywords: WEAK-WILLED AND SUBSERVIENT

Centaury is for people who find it hard to say no. They let themselves be imposed on and even bullied by others. They are usually timid, quiet, and rather passive, with little strength of will. Anxious to please, they give in to others out of subservience rather than willing co-operation. Although dissatisfied with this state of affairs, they will deny their own wishes or vocation rather than risk a confrontation. Anxious to 'do the right thing', they are easily influenced by what other people dictate.

Drained by others and out of touch with their own assertiveness, they tend to lack energy and tire easily.

The positive potential of Centaury is shown in people who serve willingly and unobtrusively, but without denying their own needs. They can express and defend their own opinions and mix well in company. Above all, they are in touch with what they want and can now follow their own path with determination and energy, unhampered by the opinions of others.

CERATO
Ceratostigma Willmottiana

Keywords: SEEKS ADVICE AND CONFIRMATION FROM OTHERS

Cerato is for people who do not trust their own judgement in decision-making. They actually know what they want and need but although they have plenty of inner wisdom and may be highly intuitive, they constantly seek advice and confirmation from others and will misguidedly follow someone else's advice rather than trust themselves. When ill, they are likely to try a succession of treatments and remedies recommended by other people.

The positive potential of Cerato is shown in those who trust their own inner wisdom and follow it. Quietly self-assured and decisive, they are able to find and follow their true vocation.

CHERRY PLUM
Prunus Cerasifera

Keywords: FEAR OF MIND GIVING WAY

Cherry Plum is indicated for people on the verge of breakdown, possibly contemplating suicide. They may be in deep despair, and afraid of losing their sanity.

Characteristically, these people are sensitive and highly strung. At times when Cherry Plum is needed they feel about to explode, and are afraid of giving way to violent impulses. Indeed they may be abnormally abusive and hysterical towards friends and family, exploding in sudden outbursts of rage.

Cherry Plum may also be indicated for screaming fits in children (*For demanding children, see Chicory and Vine*).

(If the picture is very severe, help from a good therapist is recommended).

The positive potential of Cherry Plum is the person who has a calm mind and is able to think and act rationally.

CHESTNUT BUD
Æsculus Hippocastanum

Keywords: FAILURE TO LEARN FROM PAST MISTAKES

Chestnut Bud is for failure to learn by experience, leading to an inability to make progress in life. The person keeps repeating the same mistakes, such as falling over and over again for the wrong partner, or continuing to work in an unsuitable job. Instead of learning from past difficulties, Chestnut Bud people try to forget them and therefore have no basis on which to make future decisions. They may suffer recurrent ailments but never question why they keep returning and thus fail to deal with the root cause.

Positive potential: Dr Bach wrote: 'This remedy is to help us to take full advantage of daily experiences and to see ourselves and our mistakes as others do.' The positive Chestnut Bud personality observes his or her own mistakes with objectivity, and learns from every experience, gaining knowledge and wisdom so as to move forward in life. Mentally active, he or she also observes and learns from others.

CHICORY
Cichorium intybus

Keywords: SELFISHLY POSSESSIVE

Chicory is for people who control and manipulate their loved ones; their care for others is self-centred and manipulative. These strong-willed people expect other people to conform to their values; they are critical, interfering and nagging. They are often very talkative, opinionated and argumentative.

They dislike being alone and demand constant attention and service as a duty: typical is the possessively domineering parent who keeps adult children under his or her thumb. Although strong, they are self-pitying and easily offended. When thwarted they are fretful and will give way to tears. Some Chicory people will feign illness in order to gain attention - for example, the possessive parent who manifests 'heart pains' whenever a daughter tries to leave home.

These people find it difficult not to be overly possessive, often because they have lacked genuine love in childhood.

Chicory is also good for children who make constant and unreasonable demands for attention.

The positive potential of Chicory is seen in people who are able to care for others unselfishly, offering genuine maternal love. They give without expecting anything back and allow their loved ones to be themselves and live their own lives. Feeling fulfilled and self-assured, they no longer need other people's assurance that they are worthy of love. They are warm, kind, concerned for others and sensitive to other people's needs.

CLEMATIS
Clematis Vitalba

Keywords: DREAMINESS; LACK OF INTEREST IN PRESENT

Clematis is for people who live in a world of their own with no interest in the real world. Clematis children have difficulty in concentrating, due to a tendency to daydream rather than lack of innate ability.

Preoccupied and dreamy, Clematis people are often artistic but fail to express this gift in practical, material ways. They are not really happy and yearn for better times; however they take no active steps to bring these about. They have a poor memory, with little head for detail. They fall asleep easily, sleep heavily and are often drowsy during the day. They tend to lack energy, and appear absent minded.

They like to be alone and will avoid confrontations by withdrawing. When ill they make no effort to get well. They may be strongly romantic. Clematis is appropriate for people who have lost a loved one and long to join them. Through lack of concentration, they may suffer from poor co-ordination and therefore tend to be accident-prone.

The positive potential of Clematis is a lively interest in the world around, and enjoyment of life. Positive Clematis people are open to inspiration and fulfil their creative potential, for instance in art, writing, design, fashion, or healing. Realistic and down to earth, they have a sense of purpose and recognise that the future is shaped by the present. They are well grounded and able to control their thoughts.

CRAB APPLE
Malus Pumila

Keywords: SELF-HATRED; SENSE OF UNCLEANLINESS

Crab Apple is the 'cleansing remedy' for mind and body, recommended for those who feel unclean and suffer from self-disgust. Symptoms may take the form of obsessive house-proudness, frequent hand-washing, or a mental obsession with trivialities.

Crab Apple is indicated for people who are ashamed of and embarrassed by unpleasant physical symptoms such as skin problems or discharges; they are depressed if treatment fails (*see also Gentian*). People with skin problems can use it externally, as a lotion (a few drops in water), in a compress, or added to the bath (10 drops).

The positive potential of Crab Apple is acceptance of oneself and of other people's imperfections. Positive Crab Apple people are broadminded and able to control their thoughts and deal with their difficulties.

ELM
Ulmus Procera

Keywords: OVERWHELMED BY RESPONSIBILITY

The negative Elm state is usually temporary, when people of above average ability momentarily lose confidence and become despondent. Normally capable and reliable, Elm types make good managers and are often in positions of responsibility, concerned with the welfare of others, e.g. doctors, teachers, therapists, heads of industry.

Elm is indicated when these capable people suddenly feel overwhelmed by their responsibilities and feel inadequate to deal with them or keep up with events; this is often brought about by taking on too much work without taking care of oneself. As a result they feel depressed and exhausted, with a temporary loss of self-esteem. Even a momentary doubt of their own abilities causes them to feel weak and debilitated.

The positive potential is restoration of one's normal capable personality, and a return to efficiency and self-assurance. Problems are seen in perspective and the person takes on only as much as he or she can cope with, taking time to look after his or her own needs.

GENTIAN
Gentiana Amarella

Keywords: DISCOURAGEMENT; DESPONDENCY

Gentian is for doubt and a negative outlook. Sufferers are easily discouraged and depressed when things go wrong or when faced with difficulties. Unlike Mustard, their depression is always from an identifiable cause. They may in fact be making good progress in illness or in life but are easily disheartened by small setbacks.

Gentian may be indicated for those people who feel despondent with a long-term or recurrent illness; by giving encouragement, it is often a good tonic for convalescents. It is also useful for children discouraged about their schoolwork.

The positive potential of Gentian is the realisation that there is no such thing as failure when one is doing one's best, no matter what the results. No obstacle seems too great, and no task too daunting to undertake. There is a conviction that any difficulties will be overcome in the end.

GORSE
Ulex Europaeus

Keywords: HOPELESSNESS; DESPAIR

Gorse is for extreme hopelessness and despair, for people who have given up the fight. They may be suffering from a chronic illness, and have been told that nothing more can be done to help them. Or they may believe that their illness is hereditary and therefore incurable. They feel condemned to pain and suffering and do not try to get better. They may try different treatments to please their nearest and dearest but have no faith that they will work.

Dr Bach wrote of Gorse people: 'They look as if they needed sunshine in their lives to drive the clouds away.'

The positive aspect of Gorse is a sense of faith and hope, despite current physical or mental problems. The patient feels brighter and happier and able to use illness as a positive experience. In milder cases, he or she feels on the road to recovery.

HEATHER
Calluna Vulgaris

Keywords: SELF-CENTREDNESS; SELF CONCERN

Heather is indicated for total self-preoccupation, for the type of people who are obsessed by their own ailments and problems. Often hypochondriacs, they will exaggerate their symptoms, or make mountains out of molehills. They are compulsive talkers, needing an audience and will buttonhole people in order to talk in lengthy detail about themselves. They tend to speak rapidly, close into the listener's face.

They dislike being alone but fail to realise that they are often avoided because they sap other people's vitality and show no interest in other people's problems. This self-obsession may stem from lack of love in childhood.

The positive potential of Heather is the good listener who is generous in helping others, selfless and understanding of other people's problems. Positive Heather people are able to put their own suffering to good use by empathising with others.

HOLLY
Ilex Aquifolium

Keywords: HATRED; ENVY; JEALOUSY

The negative Holly state is full of hatred, envy, and jealousy. Suffering perhaps unconsciously from insecurity, Holly people are suspicious and aggressive. They lack the ability to love and feel a generalised anger towards their fellows.

Holly people can be bad-tempered, hard-hearted, even cruel and on occasions violent. Inside, they are suffering - often for no good cause. Holly people have often lacked love in childhood and have closed up their hearts in consequence.

Holly is a good remedy for children who are jealous of their siblings. It is an important remedy for anyone interested in spiritual growth, since it opens up the capacity to give unconditional love.

The positive potential of Holly is a generous-hearted person, able to give without making demands for any return. Such people are compassionate, loving and loveable, willing to share and unpossessive, even when having personal problems themselves. Upheld by a sense of inner harmony, they take genuine pleasure in other people's success. Dr Bach wrote: 'Holly protects us from everything that is not Universal Love. Holly opens the heart and unites us with Divine Love.'

HONEYSUCKLE
Lonicera Caprifolium

Keywords: LIVES IN THE PAST

Honeysuckle is for over-attachment to past memories. It can be very helpful to bereaved or redundant people, or to those who have failed in business and especially to older people who live alone.

People in need of Honeysuckle tend to live in the past, in a state of homesickness or nostalgia. They have regrets but are unable to change present circumstances since they are constantly looking back at the past. They may be attached to lost loved ones, or to happier days, or unable to get over unhappy past experiences. They find it difficult to get over bereavement and constantly refer to the past in conversation.

The positive potential of Honeysuckle is the ability to live in the present, no longer experiencing the past as overpowering, but seeing it as valuable experience, providing lessons for today. The person can now move forward in life with no regrets. Ageing is accepted as a natural process.

HORNBEAM
Carpinus Betulus

Keywords: 'MONDAY MORNING' FEELING

Hornbeam is for weariness, mental rather than physical; for those who wake up doubting their ability to face the day's work. They find it difficult to face up to problems, or cope with the day's programme, although in fact they usually get everything done.

People in need of Hornbeam may be suffering from overwork, or a sense of staleness and lack of variety in life, for example when studying hard for exams (*see also Olive*). They lack enthusiasm and may procrastinate. Sleep is not refreshing, and if convalescing from illness, they doubt their strength to recover.

The positive potential of Hornbeam is certainty of one's strength and ability to face the day's work. A lively mind, vitality, freshness and spontaneity are restored, and life is enjoyable again. The day's work can be faced with energy and a clear head, and is properly balanced with play.

IMPATIENS
Impatiens Glandulifera

Keywords: IMPATIENCE

Impatiens is suitable for people who are easily irritated. They are impatient and nervy. The negative Impatiens character wants everything done instantly. They act, think and speak quickly, and are energetic but tense. These people are capable and efficient but irritated and frustrated by slow co-workers and therefore prefer to work alone. They are independent, hate wasting time and will finish other people's sentences.

They may have temper flare-ups but these are soon over. When ill, they make restless and irritable patients. They are often fidgety, and their hastiness may lead to accident-proneness, and poor digestion due to hasty eating.

The positive potential of Impatiens is someone who is decisive, clever and spontaneous but less hasty in thought and action. They are relaxed and good-humoured with others and sympathetic to those who are slow. They cope calmly and diplomatically with irritating problems.

LARCH
Larix Decidua

Keywords: LACK OF CONFIDENCE

Larch is for lack of self-confidence, for people who won't even try because they are sure in advance that they will fail. Although suffering from feelings of inferiority, they admire people who achieve things without envy. In fact they are secretly aware they have potential ability but refuse to acknowledge it, thereby avoiding the risk of failure. Consequently they may become discouraged and depressed.

This is also a useful remedy for anyone who lacks confidence before examinations, interviews, driving tests, etc. (*see also Rescue Remedy*).

The positive potential of Larch is expressed in people who are determined, capable, with a realistic sense of self esteem, unworried about failure or success. They are aware of their own potential and work towards achieving it. They are able to take the initiative, to take risks, and refuse to accept the word 'can't'. They use their critical faculties sensibly.

MIMULUS
Mimulus Guttatus

Keywords: FEAR OF KNOWN THINGS

Mimulus is for fear from known causes, such as: illness, death, accidents, pain, the dark, damp, cold, poverty, other people, animals, spiders, public speaking, loss of friends or job, dentistry, etc. Sufferers may be artistic and talented, but shy and retiring, and can be tongue-tied in company. Mimulus types may suffer from blushing, stammering, nervous laughter, etc.

Mimulus is good for shy, timid, sensitive children, afraid of animals, the dark, etc. *(see also Larch)*

The positive potential of Mimulus is the personality possessed of quiet courage to face trials and difficulties with humour and confidence. They can stand up for themselves, and with the emotions under complete control can enjoy life without fear. They learn to live with their sensitivity, knowing when and how to withdraw when necessary.

MUSTARD
Sinapis Arvensis

Keywords: DEEP GLOOM WITH NO ORIGIN

Mustard is for sudden depression which descends out of the blue and lifts just as suddenly for *no apparent reason*. This gloom can be very severe; it is like the descent of a cold, dark fog, overcasting everything and destroying normal cheerfulness. The sufferer is completely taken over by gloom and unable to shake it off at will.

The positive potential of Mustard is the return of joy, supported by an inner stability and peace which cannot be shaken or destroyed under good circumstances or bad.

OAK
Quercus Robur

Keywords: EXHAUSTED BUT STRUGGLES ON

Oak people are normally brave and strong; they need Oak when their inner strength wanes and fatigue takes over. They are over-achievers, who will overwork but ignore their tiredness. Driven by a strong sense of duty, they are helpful to others, conscientious and reliable. They are patient, sometimes plodding, and will not allow themselves to relax if there is work to be done; instead they struggle on obstinately when over-tired (*see also Rock-Water and Vervain*).

The resultant loss of innate strength may lead to depression, frustration and other stress symptoms, which could result in a breakdown if allowed to go on too long. These people have a sense of failure when ill but are ceaseless in their efforts to recover.

Positive potential Oak people are normally strong, often the mainstay of their family or working group. They possess enormous endurance, persistence, patience and reserves of energy, and can stand up to a good deal of stress. Oak restores their energy and helps them to recognise the need to take time off to relax and look after themselves as well as their duties.

OLIVE
Olea Europaea

Keywords: LACK OF ENERGY

Olive is for those who are spent in body and mind after a long period of strain through personal difficulties, an intense period of study or work, a long illness, or nursing someone else for a long time. It is a good remedy for convalescence.

Olive is characterised by exhaustion to the point of tears, when all reserves of strength and energy have run out. Everything is an effort; one tires easily, and life lacks zest. Sufferers no longer enjoy their work or the leisure activities in which they formerly took pleasure.

Sufferers find they need a lot of sleep. As a result of being over tired the body may be functioning below par, and a medical check-up may be advisable.

The positive potential of Olive is restoration of strength, vitality, and interest in life. Positive Olive people no longer exhaust their own reserves of strength but listen to their inner guidance and recognise the needs of their body. They are able to maintain their peace of mind even when forced to remain inactive.

PINE
Pinus Sylvestris

Keywords: SELF-REPROACH; GUILT

Pine is indicated for people who feel full of guilt and self-reproach; they blame themselves for other people's mistakes and, indeed, for anything that goes wrong. They feel undeserving and unworthy. Their guilt complex and sense of shame is not necessarily based on any actual wrong-doing but destroys the possibility of joy in living.

These people appear humble and apologetic; they will apologise for being ill and may feel they deserve their illness or pain. It should not be confused with self-disgust (*see Crab Apple*).

The positive potential of Pine is renewed energy, vitality and pleasure in living. Responsibility is accepted realistically and judgement is sound. Positive Pine people accept and respect themselves as they would others, without exaggeratedly negative judgements. In relation to Pine, Dr Bach wrote: '...One trace of condemnation against ourselves, or others, is a trace of condemnation against the Universal Creation of Love, and restricts us, limits our power to allow the Universal Love to flow through us to others.'

RED CHESTNUT
Æsculus Carnea

Keywords: FEAR OR OVER-CONCERN FOR OTHERS

Red Chestnut is for a selfless over-concern and worry for others, especially of family and close friends. They fear the worst for their loved ones: that a minor complaint will turn into something serious, that a child at play will fall, or a holiday plane will crash. They also are fretful and worry about other people's problems. It is often a temporary state among carers, nurses, counsellors, etc.

The positive potential of Red Chestnut is the ability to care for others with compassion but without anxiety. Positive Red Chestnut people radiate thoughts of health and courage to those who need them and remain mentally and physically calm in emergencies. They are happy to give help when asked but hold back from forcing help on others.

ROCK ROSE
Helianthemum Nummularium

Keywords: TERROR

Rock Rose is for terror such as may occur after being in an accident or having a near escape, or from witnessing an accident. When under acute threat - such as a natural disaster, sudden illness, a mugging, etc., there is a sense of frozen fear and helplessness.

A similar state of terror may occur as the result of nightmares (*see also Rescue Remedy*).

The Rock Rose state is usually brief, related to a particular crisis.

The positive potential of Rock Rose is courage and presence of mind; the person who is calm and self-forgetful in emergencies.

ROCK WATER
Aqua Petra

Keywords: SELF REPRESSION, SELF DENIAL

Rock Water is for inflexibility: it is indicated for people who may be self-denying but at the same time over-concentrated on themselves. They are self-dominating to the point of self-martyrdom. They will stick rigidly to diet and exercise programmes, work routines and spiritual disciplines. They are opinionated; their thinking is ruled by fixed ideas and dogma regarding subjects like religion, diet, morality, politics, etc. They like to set an example to others but because they seek self-perfection, do not actively interfere in other people's lives.

These people are over-conscientious and set high standards for themselves. They often overwork but are never satisfied with their own achievements. They are self-sacrificing and denying and feel disappointed with themselves if they do not meet their own high ideals.

The positive potential of Rock Water is expressed in the ability to hold high ideals with a flexible mind. Positive Rock Water people are willing to change their minds and give up their pet theories if convinced of a greater truth. They understand that inner harmony is more powerful than externally enforced behaviour and allow themselves more flow in life.

SCLERANTHUS
Scleranthus Annuus

Keywords: UNCERTAINTY, INDECISION

Scleranthus is for people who suffer indecision: people in need of Scleranthus find it difficult to make decisions, particularly when faced with a choice of two possibilities. These people lack balance and poise; their grasshopper minds make them jump about in conversation. They are up and down in mood, experiencing extremes of joy/sadness, energy/apathy, optimism/pessimism, laughing/crying. This changeable outlook can make them unreliable and they can waste time and lose opportunities due to indecision.

Scleranthus is recommended for children who suffer from travel sickness.

The positive potential of Scleranthus is certainty and decisiveness, with poise and balance in all circumstances. Positive Scleranthus people are able to make quick decisions and act promptly when necessary.

STAR OF BETHLEHEM
Ornithogalum umbellatum

Keywords: AFTER EFFECTS OF SHOCK

Star of Bethlehem is for the after-effects of shock, mental or physical as a result of accidents, bad news, bereavement, sudden disappointments, frights etc. It is an important ingredient of the Rescue Remedy. It is useful for both mother and child immediately after a birth.

Although ideally taken immediately after the event, it is also excellent for delayed effects which may manifest years after the event in the form of physical symptoms. People may be numbed and withdrawn with a sense of loss or grief.

The positive effect of Star of Bethlehem is to neutralise the effects of the shock, whether immediate or delayed, thus helping the sufferer to recuperate.

Dr Bach described this remedy as 'the comforter and soother of pains and sorrows'.

SWEET CHESTNUT
Castanea Sativa

Keywords: EXTREME MENTAL ANGUISH

Sweet Chestnut is for agonising mental anguish, described by Dr Bach as 'the hopeless despair of those who feel they have reached the limit of their endurance.' It may take the form of intense sorrow; sufferers can feel almost destroyed by it. Dejection accompanied by a sense of loneliness and the feeling that the future is bleak and utterly hopeless.

They may feel on the point of nervous breakdown, though not suicidal. There may be the feeling that God has forsaken them.

This state may follow a bereavement, or years of difficulty, suffered bravely and uncomplainingly.

The positive potential of Sweet Chestnut is liberation from despair and despondency. Though external circumstances may not have changed, they can now be faced with optimism and peace of mind. This may be aided by the discovery or recovery of faith in a higher power and a sense of inner support.

VERVAIN
Verbena Officinalis

Keywords: OVER-ENTHUSIASM

Vervain is for those with fixed principles and ideas, which they are confident are right and which they rarely change; subjects are determined but highly strung, over-achieving and keyed-up. They put unnecessary effort into everything they undertake, pushing themselves beyond their physical limits. Their minds race ahead of events; they take on too much work and try to tackle too many jobs at once.

These people are strong-willed and hold strong views. Sensitive to injustice and dedicated to causes, often self-sacrificially, their over-enthusiasm can be fanatical, so that they alienate potential allies and converts.

They may suffer from lack of sleep due to their active minds and inability or unwillingness to relax. Demonstrative in speech and movement, they can be irritable, frustrated and annoyed over matters of principle.

The positive potential of Vervain is the person who is calm, wise, tolerant and able to relax. Although they hold strong views, they can change them when appropriate and do not need to impose them on others. They take a broad view of life and events.

Positive Vervain people understand, as Dr Bach wrote: 'It is by being rather than doing that great things are accomplished.'

VINE
Vitis Vinifera

Keywords: DOMINEERING; INFLEXIBLE

Vine is for people who dominate others. They are often very capable, even highly gifted and ambitious but they use their undoubted gifts to dominate and bully. They know better than everyone else and put other people down. Although they do not try to convert other people they override their wishes and opinions and demand and expect absolute obedience.

They are aggressive and proud and can be ruthlessly greedy for power; the extremes are hard, cruel and uncompassionate. Extreme examples are the parent or boss who rules with an iron rod, or the political dictator who uses any means to gain his ends, or the school bully who aggressively controls other children.

The positive potential of Vine is determination without domination. Positive Vine people see the good in others and encourage and guide without controlling them.

They make wise, loving leaders, teachers, bosses or parents. They use their gifts to help others to know themselves and find their own path in life. They inspire others with their unshakeable confidence and certainty.

WALNUT
Juglans Regia

Keywords: PROTECTION FROM CHANGE AND OUTSIDE INFLUENCES

Walnut protects against the effects of over-sensitivity to certain ideas, atmospheres and influences. It is the remedy for times of major life changes - teething, puberty, pregnancy, divorce, menopause; changes of religion; moving a job or home; giving up an addiction or breaking away from old ties and restrictions; also for the regrets caused by change - loss of friends and familiar circumstances, ageing, bereavement, approaching death, etc. (*see also Honeysuckle*).

Those in need of Walnut have definite ideals and ambitions and are keen to move forward in life but are held back or side-tracked by the influence of a stronger personality, by restrictive circumstances, by family ties or links with the past. They may be temporarily affected by another's personality or problems: it is useful for therapists, healers and counsellors dealing with emotionally troubled or draining clients. It is the remedy that provides constancy and protection from the influence of others.

The positive potential of Walnut is the ability to move forward and remain steadfast to one's path in life, free of the past, and to make necessary changes in life, carrying plans through despite discouragement, objections or ridicule from others.

WATER VIOLET
Hottonia Palustris

Keywords: PROUD; ALOOF

The Water Violet type is knowledgeable, calm, and capable. They are private, sedate people, who are often asked for advice but will not impose their opinions or wishes on others. Gentle and self-reliant, they have a sense of superiority which is actually well-founded. However, carried to extremes, they can be aloof, appearing proud, disdainful and condescending. When they are tired, or there are too many external distractions, they have a tendency to withdraw, appearing anti-social and cold.

When suffering they keep their troubles to themselves. They do not lean on others for support and may be considered emotionally cold.

The positive potential of Water Violet is a warmer relationship with others, while maintaining one's wisdom and dignity. Water Violet people are happy to help others with the benefit of their own knowledge and wisdom. Calm, serene, dignified, they are able to understand and empathise with others. They often put their talents to the service of others, as counsellors or teachers for example.

WHITE CHESTNUT
Æsculus Hippocastanum

Keywords: UNWANTED THOUGHTS; MENTAL ARGUMENTS

White Chestnut is indicated for obsessive, worrying thoughts that seem impossible to control. Sufferers cannot let go of unhappy events or arguments and keep reliving them mentally.

Persistent, unwanted thoughts and mental arguments go round and round like a stuck record, leading to a troubled mind and depression. It is difficult to concentrate during the day, or to sleep at night. The sufferer may therefore appear inattentive and may not answer when spoken to (*see also Clematis*).

The positive potential of White Chestnut is peace of mind. The head is clear; thinking is under control and can be put to positive use in problem-solving. Worry is replaced by trust in a positive outcome.

WILD OAT
Bromus Ramosus

Keywords: UNCERTAINTY AS TO CORRECT PATH IN LIFE

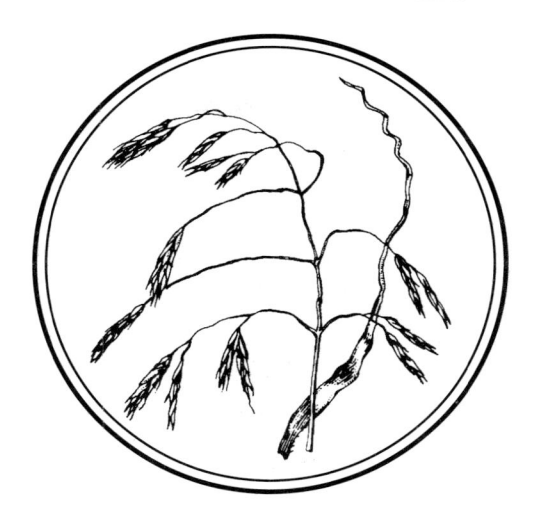

Wild Oat is helpful in making important decisions such as choosing a career. Unlike Scleranthus, which involves a choice between (usually) two decisions, Wild Oat is for people who have reached a cross-roads in life and are completely undecided as to what to do. They may have ambition and a variety of talents but waste their gifts through lack of a clear direction. They may try several different careers but easily become bored and unsettled, tending to be drifters. They are often unconventional. At the same time they are aware that life is passing them by and feel frustrated and dissatisfied (*see also Cerato and Seleranthus*).

The positive potential of Wild Oat is a clear picture of what to do in life, with positive ideas and ambitions, and the ability to decide upon one's true path. Talents are used constructively. These multi-talented people may find ways of pursuing more than one career at once. They no longer give up when bored.

WILD ROSE
Rosa Canina

Keywords: RESIGNATION; APATHY

Wild Rose is indicated for anyone who is resigned to an unpleasant situation, whether illness, a monotonous life or uncongenial work. They do not complain but are too apathetic to get well, change their occupation or enjoy simple pleasures. Although their situations are unsatisfactory, they are not actually unhappy and make no effort to change their circumstances. This makes them rather dull as companions, and unable to fulfil their potential.

When ill, they are over-accepting of medical prognoses such as 'you must learn to live with it'. They may believe that their condition is hereditary and therefore that nothing further can be done. They are resigned, rather than depressed, at the prospect and accept life the way it is. They lack energy and ambition and may speak in a monotonous voice.

They fail to realise that one's attitude creates one's life conditions and contributes to health and success.

The positive potential of Wild Rose is a lively interest in life, work and the world in general. Resignation gives way to ambition and a sense of purpose, good health and enjoyable friendships. Positive Wild Rose people accept responsibility for their own lives and circumstances and use their initiative to make changes.

WILLOW
Salix Vitellina

Keywords: RESENTMENT

Willow is for resentment, self-pity and bitterness. Most people feel more or less put-upon at times; this remedy helps to neutralise resentment and regain a sense of humour and proportion.

Willow is for feelings of being short-changed by life - 'I don't deserve this. Why should it happen to me?' The person in the negative Willow state begrudges other people's good luck, health, happiness or success. They are grumbling, sulky and irritable and enjoy spreading gloom. They are only interested in other people in order to decry and criticise. They take without giving, and without gratitude, alienating their friends and family.

These people make difficult patients when ill, since they are never pleased or satisfied, preferring to see themselves as victims and reluctant to admit to any improvement. Constantly maintaining resentment can affect one's overall vitality and lead to poor general health.

The positive potential of Willow is a state of optimism and faith. The positive Willow person recognises that the power of thought creates one's own circumstances. They are able to forgive and forget past injustices and enjoy life, thereby attracting positive conditions and friends. No longer victims, they are in control of their own destiny.

RESCUE REMEDY

Dr Bach created an emergency combination which he called Rescue Remedy. It contains five flower remedies: Impatiens, Star of Bethlehem; Cherry Plum, Rock Rose and Clematis. It is worth carrying a small bottle with you in case of emergencies.

A Rescue Remedy cream with added Crab Apple is available as a multi-purpose skin salve for external application.

For demanding and stressful situations

Rescue Remedy is the remedy to be used in emergencies. If you have received sudden bad news, a family upset or a bereavement; if you are fearful, confused, or even in terror, Rescue Remedy will help you face the situation in a better frame of mind.

It can also be taken before a stressful event: for example, while waiting for important news; prior to sitting an exam or taking a driving test; before a difficult meeting or interview; before going on stage or giving a speech; before going to the dentist or into hospital. Rescue Remedy will help to reduce your fear and nervousness.

It is an excellent remedy whenever you feel uptight or unduly bothered, and can usually restore balance.

On occasions when your mind is over-active, take a dose or two in the evening before going to sleep.

After an accident, an immediate dose of Rescue Remedy can contribute greatly to counteracting its effects and helping the natural healing process to take its course. If there has been an accident at home, out of doors or on the road, those involved may be experiencing confusion. While waiting for medical help the Rescue Remedy can be used to relieve the fear of both victim and onlookers and provide comfort and reassurance.

Note: Like all the flower remedies, Rescue Remedy is not intended to replace medical treatment but is an invaluable support while waiting for medical help in an emergency. It is natural, entirely safe and gentle, is not habit forming and will not interfere with any other medical treatment.

Dosage for Rescue Remedy

If there is no water or other liquid to hand, the patient can be given drops direct from the stock bottle. (**N.B. This should be done with caution: since all the remedies are preserved in brandy, this entails a direct intake of alcohol, which may not be acceptable for everyone for religious or other reasons.**)

External application

Rescue Remedy can be diluted and used as a lotion. A couple of undiluted drops can be used direct from the bottle unless the skin is severely broken.

Rescue Remedy cream can be applied as a multi-purpose skin salve for external applications. It can also be used preventively in advance of, say, strenuous exercise.

RECOMMENDED BOOKS: *Rescue Remedy* (Vlamis)
(See pages 54 - 56)   *Questions & Answers* (Ramsell)

CHOOSING REMEDIES FOR CHILDREN

Childbirth

After birth, a combination of Rescue Remedy and Walnut is particularly useful. Star of Bethlehem and Walnut can be given to both mother and child after a difficult labour. In neutralising any negative feelings the mother may be subject to, she will also benefit her child.

Childhood problems

Babies and children can be given the remedies with complete safety and very good results. Children and babies suffer from many emotions and go through times of stress and unhappiness; dealing with these in childhood can help them to grow up happily and healthily.

The remedies should be chosen for children in exactly the same way as for adults. Whether the child is suffering from a physical illness, or is fretful, unhappy, or difficult for no obvious reason, his or her personality and current characteristics are the guide to the required remedy or combination of remedies.

The dosage is also the same as for adults: two drops prepared with boiled water for babies, and given with milk, water or fruit juice. When the baby is being breast-fed, it is sufficient for the mother to take the remedy. The dosage should be repeated four times a day until the child has recovered.

There are countless childhood situations for which particular remedies have been found to be very effective. For example, children who demand constant attention may be of a Chicory or Vine nature. Those who are inclined to day-dream may require Clematis. Shy, nervous, timid children would be suggestive of a Mimulus personality. Holly would help children who are jealous, Honeysuckle for those who feel homesick, for example while at boarding school. It must be remembered, however, that one cannot generalise, so it is important to consider each child's needs individually.

RECOMMENDED BOOKS: *Bach Flower Remedies for Women* (Howard)
(See pages 54 - 56) *Growing Up with Bach Flower Remedies* (Howard)

CHOOSING REMEDIES FOR ANIMALS AND PLANTS

Assess the characteristics of the animal exactly as for a person. Drops of the remedy can be given on food or in the animal's drinking water; two drops for birds and small animals, ten drops in a bucket of water for large animals.

Plants can benefit from Rescue Remedy and/or Walnut after transplanting. Other Remedies of particular value are Crab Apple combined with Rescue Remedy for pest infestations and Hornbeam, Olive and/or Gorse to invigorate limp plants.

RECOMMENDED BOOKS: *Questions & Answers* (Ramsell)
(See pages 54 - 56)   *The Bach Flower Remedies Step by Step* (Howard)
   Rescue Remedy (Vlamis)

FURTHER INFORMATION

This booklet is intended to provide a general introduction to the work of Dr Edward Bach. For those who wish to gain a more comprehensive understanding of the subject the following literature is recommended:

Practical information

The Twelve Healers & Other Remedies - *Edward Bach, C.W. Daniel Co. Ltd., 1933*
This is Dr Bach's own simple and clear explanation of each of the flower remedy states. It is the definitive text and therefore the most essential.

The Bach Flower Remedies Step by Step - *Judy Howard, C.W. Daniel Co. Ltd., 1990*
A complete practical guide to choosing and using the remedies. It contains full descriptions of each remedy, and includes detailed advice on selecting remedies for oneself, one's family, friends and clients, recognising type remedies, consultations, treating animals and plants, the preparation and administration of the remedies.

The Dictionary of the Bach Flower Remedies - *Tom Hyne-Jones, C.W. Daniel Co. Ltd.*
A quick reference guide with key sentences to describe the positive and negative aspects of each remedy.

Handbook of the Bach Flower Remedies - *Philip M. Chancellor, C.W. Daniel Co. Ltd., 1971*
Each remedy description is supplemented by several case histories which help the learner appreciate their use. It is a comprehensive book and an aid to understanding the remedies in more depth. (Illustrated with colour prints of each remedy flower).

The Bach Remedies Repertory - *F.J. Wheeler, C.W. Daniel Co. Ltd., 1952*
This lists various moods or states of mind and gives suggested remedies which may be appropriate. Must be used in conjunction with a book which provides the individual descriptions.

Bach Flower Remedies for Women - *Judy Howard, C.W. Daniel Co. Ltd., 1992*
An open account of womanhood and the trials encountered by women of all ages. This book provides constructive advice on how the Bach remedies can be used at different stages of a woman's life. Subjects include: menstruation and pre-menstrual tension, pregnancy, childbirth, infertility, screening procedures (e.g. breast and cervical), dieting, sexual difficulties, ill-health (e.g. M.E., irritable bowel), menopause, ageing, widowhood and loneliness.

Growing Up with Bach Flower Remedies - *Judy Howard, C.W. Daniel Co. Ltd., 1994*
How the remedies can help children, adolescents and their parents. This book describes the various potentially traumatic periods of a child's life and how the remedies can help. Subjects discussed include: behavioural difficulties, feeding, sleeping, going to school, shyness, puberty, learning difficulties, examinations, relationships etc. A reference book for parents and anyone involved in caring for children of all ages.

Questions & Answers - *John Ramsell, C.W. Daniel Co. Ltd., 1986*
This book, written by John Ramsell who worked alongside Dr Bach's colleagues Nora Weeks and Victor Bullen, offers a wealth of helpful information. It incorporates chapters on the principles of the Bach method, remedy comparisons and special needs, as well as a host of other practical advice.

Bach Flower Therapy: Theory & Practice - *Mechthild Scheffer, Thorsons, 1990*
This book provides helpful and comprehensive descriptions of each remedy, together with psychological and spiritual considerations.

Rescue Remedy - *Gregory Vlamis, Thorsons, 1986*
A collection of case histories and testimonies about the use of the Rescue Remedy for adults, children, animals and plants, submitted by doctors, vets, holistic therapists, practitioners and lay people from around the world.

Philosophy, history & general interest

Heal Thyself - *Edward Bach, C.W. Daniel Co. Ltd., 1931*
This is Dr Bach's philosophy and describes Dr Bach's belief regarding the true cause of disease, the basis on which the remedies were developed. Essential reading.

Medical Discoveries of Edward Bach Physician - *Nora Weeks, C.W. Daniel Co. Ltd., 1940*
Dr Bach's biography, written by his successor who devoted her life to Bach's work. It explains in detail Dr Bach's career as a physician, bacteriologist and homoeopath and follows him on his subsequent journey to find the flower remedies.

The Original Writings of Edward Bach - *compiled from the archives of the Bach Centre by its curators and trustees - Judy Howard and John Ramsell, C.W. Daniel Co. Ltd., 1990*
This book gives readers a chance to share Dr Bach's most inspirational writings and stories. It provides insight into his thoughts, contains early work connected to his findings, lectures, letters, case notes, character descriptions by his friends and colleagues and some early photographs.

The Story of Mount Vernon - *Judy Howard, 1987*
Dr Bach lived at Mount Vernon during the last years of his life and this was where his work was finalised. Since his death, Mount Vernon has remained the centre of his work, and is known as The Bach Centre. This book tells of how Bach's work continued since he came to live at Mount Vernon.

An Introduction to the Benefits of the Bach Flower Remedies - *Jane Evans, C.W. Daniel Co. Ltd., 1977*
This booklet provides the beginner with an account of how the remedies can become a way of life.

The Bach Flower Remedies, Illustrations & Preparations - *Nora Weeks & Victor Bullen, C.W. Daniel Co. Ltd., 1964*
A book for those who have a botanical interest in the plants used for remedy preparation.

Video & audio cassette tapes

VIDEO: The Light that never goes out, 1992
This film tells the story of Dr Bach's life and work. It follows his progress as a physician in bacteriology and homeopathy, and the development of his discovery over the subsequent six years leading to its conclusion, completion and continuation to this day from his home Mount Vernon, the Bach Centre. *Running time: 38 minutes*

VIDEO: The Bach Flower Remedies; A Further Understanding - 1993
Filmed at Mount Vernon, this video is a general guide to using the remedies, covering many of the difficulties and confusions people have raised over the years. The Trustees of Mount Vernon, John Ramsell and Judy Howard, discuss many aspects of the remedies and give simple guidelines for the benefit of those wishing to help themselves and others. *Running time: 68 minutes*

AUDIO CASSETTE: Getting to Know the Bach Flower Remedies
The Bach Centre provides straightforward, clear and concise descriptions of each remedy, with helpful examples and practical exercises for the listener.
75 minutes approx.

COMPLETE READING LIST

Video: The Light that Never Goes Out
Video: The Bach Flower Remedies: - Further Understanding
Audio Cassette: Getting to Know the Bach Flower Remedies
The Twelve Healers & Other Remedies
The Bach Flower Remedies Step by Step
Questions & Answers
Handbook of the Bach Flower Remedies
Bach Flower Remedies for Women
Growing Up with Bach Flower Remedies
Medical Discoveries of Edward Bach
Heal Thyself
Original Writings of Edward Bach
Story of Mount Vernon
Dictionary of the Bach Flower Remedies
Bach Remedies Repertory
Benefits of the Bach Flower Remedies
Bach Flower Remedies
Illustrations & Preparations
Pictorial Reference Cards
Bach Flower Therapy: Theory and Practice
Rescue Remedy

These publications are all available by mail order from the Dr Edward Bach Centre (see below), or from your local book shop, health food store or pharmacist.

The Dr Edward Bach Centre,
Mount Vernon,
Sotwell,
Wallingford,
Oxon OX10 0PZ
Tel: 01491 834678